WORDS OF LIFE

ART INSPIRED DEVOTIONAL

ALLISON TEAL LEWIS

WORDS OF LIFE DEVOTIONAL

ACKNOWLEDGMENTS

Above all I want to thank the Holy Spirit, without whom you would have nothing to see here. I also thank God for my amazingly supportive other half, Daniel, who is the best partner I could ask for in going after our dreams together. A special thanks to Joanna Hess, Kristi Ahrens, Bridget Myers, and Tami Demers for editing and helping me see this project of love off the ground. Finally, I want to thank you for joining me on this monthly journey of connection with our Creator.

CONTENTS

INTRODUCTION

This twelve-entry devotional is designed to help you focus your heart on the encouragement God wants to bring you through one artwork a month. This booklet was originally written as a companion to a calendar. The same artworks have been used in this devotional, but revised and edited to be used as a simple devotional not limited to one specific year. This devotional is different than many daily devotional works available. I believe the power behind focusing on one artwork and specific questions per month gives the heart and mind a chance to rest and recalibrate in the truth one encounters. This time also allows you to process and implement the question/answer portion at the end of each section. The invitation is to savor each month without rushing into the next. See what deeper work God desires to produce in your life as you marinate on each one. I pray that you are blessed to be a blessing!

-Allison

JANUARY

The Lord is my best friend and my shepherd. I always have more than enough.

Psalm 23:1

The mature children of God are those who are moved by the impulses of the Holy Spirit. And you did not receive the spirit of religious duty, leading you back into the fear of never being good enough. But you have received the Spirit of full acceptance, enfolding you into the family of God. And you will never feel orphaned, for as he rises up within us, our spirits join him in saying the words of tender affection, "Beloved Father!" For the Holy Spirit makes God's fatherhood real to us as he whispers into our innermost being, "You are God's beloved child!"

Romans 8:14-16

If I really believed this, how would my life be different?

I bless you at the beginning of this year with knowing He is your "enough," and you are enough for Him, just as you are. Wherever you find yourself struggling to accept this truth, I pray the journey takes you to new places you never thought were possible in your relationship with God. Our Shepherd that leads us by still waters does not wait for the enemies to flee to provide enough. He is so fully confident in His care over us that He serves up a feast in front of them. In the midst of this year that can appear to loom with discouragement and destruction, He is yet preparing a table before you. Feast on His goodness as you focus your days on His face. He is enough, and you are enough to Him.

In this specific art piece, the blue represents Holy Spirit as an incubator. A safe place to harbor, surrounded by gold that reflects God's refining and enduring love. All of this is more fully realized and accepted when we reach a place of surrender, humility, and value. This humility and surrender by the individual is represented by the color brown that were used for the letters of "Enough." He surrounds us with all we need as we surrender to His voice and comfort.

HEART RESPONSE;

- Ask God to show you if there are any lies you are believing that are blocking your heart from receiving the truth of these verses.

- Give them to God and ask Him to replace them with truth.

- Journal or share with a trusted friend how your life would be different if these truths were really real! Ask this friend to bless you or pray for you about this truth. This requires vulnerability. You might not feel ready for that. That is just fine!

- Thank God for the truth and notice this month when you need to remind yourself of it again. This is renewing your mind so it will not be a one-time exercise! Every time you replace a lie with truth you create a new brain pathway. This new mind "roadway" is ready to drive on, but you have to use it!

He will
exult over you with joy
He will quiet you by his love
He will

rejoice

OVER *you*
with shouts of joy

ZEPHANIAH 3:17

FEBRUARY

The Lord your God is in your midst, a mighty one who will save. He will rejoice over you with gladness; he will quiet you by his love; he will rejoice over you with shouts of joy.

Zephaniah 3:17

I was curious about the phrase, "quiet you" with His love. What was found completely surprised me. According to Strong's Bible Concordance, the term is more literally translated, "to MAKE silent/quiet/ almost deaf," with His loud shouts of joy and overpowering love. A statement to show the force of His love causes an awe similar to standing in front of Niagara Falls! This is not the type of rejoicing that quiets us down like a crying baby. I do believe He communicates that as well, but not in this context. He is making a point.

Take that in. Notice how this verse makes you feel or what it makes you think of. Have you ever felt God's loud joy and approval over you like this? If so, focus on that experience today. Think of it every time you look at this image.

Sense God as a proud, brand new Father holding His baby for the first time. How does that make you feel, knowing you are His prized daughter or son? He cannot wait to shout from the rooftops, "She's mine!" or "Did you see my son yet?!" Before a baby has the time to deserve any kind of applause, in a healthy environment they are simply celebrated. His joy over us becomes our foundation and fountain of strength.

In this painting I chose to represent God's intimate and passionate love for His sons and daughters by using the color pink. The deep blue of the word "rejoice" reminds viewers of the deep strength of His joy over us. It is never ending and deeper than the ocean floor. Again, gold represents the eternal quality of His love for us and the faithfulness of His commitment to us as a perfect Father.

HEART RESPONSE

- Draw, journal, meditate, or share with someone today this concept of how much joy you bring the Father, just by existing, and how that is true of them too.

- How does your heart accept or reject that truth? There is no place for guilt or condemnation or shame if it is difficult. See it as a red flag to do whatever it takes to receive it and know it is available to you now.

- Ask God to show you any lie or memory that might be in the way of your whole heart accepting this truth. Picture yourself placing the lie or memory in the Father's hands and taking the love He offers in exchange.

- If you already see yourself as the rejoiced over son or daughter you are, simply spend time praising Him. If you are bubbling over with this truth, you could make a goal of sharing this every day this month with someone you meet.

i will give you

Beauty

for ashes

the oil of joy for mourning

the garment of praise

for the spirit of heaviness

MARCH

The spirit of the Sovereign Lord is on me, because the Lord has anointed me to proclaim good news to the poor. He has sent me to bind up the brokenhearted, to proclaim freedom for the captives and release from darkness for the prisoners, to proclaim the year of the Lord's favor and the day of vengeance of our God, to comfort all who mourn, and provide for those who grieve in Zion- to bestow on them a crown of beauty instead of ashes, the oil of joy instead of mourning, and a garment of praise instead of a spirit of despair. They will be called oaks of righteousness, a planting of the Lord for the display of his splendor.

Isaiah 61

Where is the place you have seen ashes this year? Where are you waiting for beauty to show up? Ask God to bring to mind a picture or word of hope that will help you in the waiting to see this beauty spring up.

We all know this year has seen its share of ashes, but for those still waiting for beauty to sprout, sometimes hope needs planting for Him to be able to water it. This month every time you see this image of fire poppies, (an actual variety of flower that only grows in the aftermath of a wildfire) when you are tempted to walk down the familiar road of discouragement- remember what He showed you. Cling to it like treasure, like fire poppy seeds buried deep in the waiting for just the right moment to bloom.

HEART RESPONSE

- Write down or draw your picture of hope. Share with a friend what He brings to mind, knowing there are souls all around you who need what you have.

- When you see even a glimmer of beauty or sprout of His redemption of a specific area in your life that was bare, SHARE it! Write it out. Praise Him! Watch how it multiplies seeds of hope to others, as yours returns.

APRIL

He who dwells in the secret place of the Most High shall abide under the shadow of the Almighty. I will say of the Lord, "He is my refuge and my fortress; My God, in Him I will trust."

Psalm 91: 1,2

I am the sprouting vine and you're my branches. As you live in union with me as your source, fruitfulness will stream from within you-but when you live separated from me you are powerless.

John 15:5

According to Biblehub.com, "abide" has two different meanings in these passages. Each has beautiful significance of its own for our daily lives. Abide found in Psalm 91 has the transliteral meaning of "to lodge, to stay the night, to shelter." The white Abide word on the art piece shouts brightly, "I'm here! I am choosing to be here. To stay the night, riding out the storm with you." The word is also requesting the viewer to abide as well. The other meaning of abide, found in the vine passage in John, refers to a longer "dwelling, staying, remaining in." This is represented from me in this painting as the pinkish purple color of juice and fruit, surrounding the word Abide. God knows we need both; the temporal shelter from circumstances and storms that pass over us, and the constant need for His grace to grow in Him.

How do you know you are abiding? What does a moment or day of abiding feel like? What seems to steal your ability to abide? What keeps you from getting rid of those hindrances? Are there people or circumstances in your life that you have no control over, that seem to threaten your ability to abide? Take this moment to ask God to show you how to think differently about them. What does abiding in Him looks like in a particular circumstance. Stay awhile until He speaks to your heart. Believe if it is encouraging, and true to His character and word, He is speaking to you!

HEART RESPONSE

- Write down what God showed you or spoke to your heart about how to think differently.

- Share what God showed you with a trusted friend or family member.

- Every time you come across this artwork, or simply the word "abide," thank God for the daily, sustaining, strength and protection He offers you. He is amazing!

- Watch your level of peace rise as you abide. Consider drawing a picture or journaling of your experience this month.

psalm 33:11

The
Purposes
of the Lord
stand forever

MAY

Words He breathed and worlds were birthed.

"Let there be," and "there is" was springing forth the moment He spoke. No sooner said than done! With His breath He scatters the schemes of nations who oppose Him; they will never succeed. His destiny-plan for the earth stands sure. His forever-plan remains in place and will never fail.

Psalm 33:9-12

For I know the thoughts that I think toward you, says the LORD, thoughts of peace and not of evil, to give you a future and a hope.

Jeremiah 29:11

So why would I fear the future? For your goodness and love pursue me all the days of my life. Then afterward, when my life is through, I'll return to your glorious presence to be forever with you!

Psalm 23:6

What news headline or circumstance in your life most challenges your security and trust in God's purposes? Are you ready to surrender that on the altar of your heart, in exchange for His peace over the future? He is so patient and kind! He is capable, trustworthy, and waiting.

The blue and purple colors in this piece are intended to stir up hope, while the silver communicates redemption and words of life that shine like silver compared with the negativity we are surrounded by. The tree is unique and snuck into this piece because trees always represent a strength and trust in the Lord to me. His love roots go deep in our hearts to help us hold on to hope in the times it is threatened.

HEART RESPONSE

- Which of these verses I shared are most difficult for you to grab onto fully? Ask God why. Write down the answer. If you are ready, surrender that answer and ask God to replace it with the truth about Himself. Ask for His strength to fully embrace it. Share this process with a friend to experience authentic connection and community. Your freedom might become theirs as well!

- Write out a declaration of truth over current or future circumstances that you need hope for. Place this in a strategic place you will see every day or write it under the art for this month. Speak this truth out loud everyday this month.

Act justly

Love

MERCY

walk humbly
with your God

MICAH 6:8

JUNE

He has shown you O mortal, what is good. And what does the Lord require of you? To act justly and to love mercy and to walk humbly with your God.

Micah 6:8

The steadfast love of the Lord never ceases; his mercies never come to an end; they are new every morning; great is your faithfulness.

"The Lord is my inheritance" says my soul, "therefore I will hope in Him."

Lamentations 3:22-24

Mercy triumphs over judgement.

James 2:13

Be merciful, even as your Father is merciful.

Luke 6:36

So speak and so act as those who are to be judged under the law of liberty.

James 2:12

I remember growing up with this verse on a little magnet stuck to my parents top/ bottom cream-colored refrigerator in the 80's. Every time I went to get a glass of milk from the fridge, or came home from school passing through the kitchen, it was burned into the fibers of my heart a little more. You never know what is going to "stick" in your child's heart or those around you!

If you know me for any length of time you will find out I have a passion for the end of human trafficking and modern-day slavery. But really any issue of justice burns in my heart alongside our mandate to be agents of reconciliation that Paul talks about in 2 Corinthians. It's with this desire for justice I made this piece in particular. I felt so passionate in creating it, while remembering the verse I saw all those years ago on our fridge. Did that plant something in me that wouldn't have been there before, or was it just stirring something He put in me from birth? Kind of like the question, "Which came first, the chicken or the egg?" I suppose. Either way, it fascinates me how God can use just one verse, or word to inspire our hearts and fuel our decisions and imaginations. I am sure each person reading this has a story of their own about a word or verse that directed the course of their life.

As I was creating this piece with a rainbow of colors, I felt that the focus word needed to be love, and not justice. The only way we can see true justice that flows from what Christ did on the cross, is to have eyes, lenses of love and mercy to see through. We need a recalibration of our hearts and new understanding of God's definition of mercy and justice, if we are to ever see it manifest in our church and society. Only He has the ability to create solutions of justice more beautiful than all the colors around His throne.

HEART RESPONSE

- Journal; What is one area of your life that needs mercy? Where is one situation where you are waiting for justice?

- Draw or share with a friend what it looks like to walk humbly with the God of mercy AND justice into that place.

- Rather than seeing a contradiction in the meanings of justice and mercy, ask God to realign your heart to His definitions. Take this month to look out for HIS ways of mercy and justice, allowing Him to make adjustments in your thinking and choices.

JULY

Hope deferred makes the heart sick, but a longing fulfilled is a tree of life.

Proverbs 13:12

Now may God, the inspiration and fountain of hope, fill you to overflowing with uncontainable joy and perfect peace as you trust in Him. And may the power of the Holy Spirit continually surround your life with His superabundance until you radiate with hope!

Romans 15:13

Celebrate with praises the God and Father of our Lord Jesus Christ, who has shown us His extravagant mercy. For His fountain of mercy has given us a new life-we are reborn to experience a living, energetic hope through the resurrection of Jesus Christ from the dead. We are reborn into a perfect inheritance that can never perish, never be defiled, and never diminish. It is promised and preserved forever in the heavenly realm for you!

1 Peter 1:3

Hope deferred makes the heart sick. A heart full of praise set on His goodness has room for nothing less than a tree of life. When we have Him, we have hope Himself living inside us. One of my favorites, yet most convicting quotes, is from Steve Backlund with Igniting Hope Ministries;

"Every area of your life that isn't glistening with hope, you're believing a lie."

Ouch! This month take time to ask God to highlight any area of your life you are feeling discouraged in and have given up hope. Hand it over to Him, and ask Him to replace the lie about your circumstance that there is no hope anymore for this situation or person. I have also heard it said, "There are no hopeless circumstances, only hopeless people." Ask God to replace your hopelessness with the truths about His goodness and His ability to be at work in every circumstance for His glory, and your good. If the situation isn't full of hope yet, God is not done with it. We can't afford to have a thought about ourselves that God doesn't have. He has no hopeless thoughts about your life.

HEART RESPONSE

- As crazy as it might sound to your mind right now, dream about what your day would look like if you had "glistening hope" about EVERY area of your life. Wherever that feels impossible, ask God to show you the way out. Any thought that doesn't line up with God's goodness is stealing the freedom He died to give you.

- As you return to the artwork for this month, remember the places God has saved your thinking. Thank Him for new hope in that area. Share with a friend or write a declaration of hope under this month's art, about that person or circumstance.

out of the

Overflow

of the HEART
the mouth SPEAKS

AUGUST

I overflow with praise when I come before you, for the anointing of your presence satisfies me like nothing else. You are such a rich banquet of pleasure to my soul.

Psalm 63:5

Be filled with the fullness of the Holy Spirit. And your hearts will overflow with a joyful song to the Lord. Keep speaking to each other with words of Scripture, singing the Psalms with praises and spontaneous songs given by the Spirit!

Ephesians 5:18,19

Above all else, guard your heart, for everything you do flows from it.

Proverbs 4:23

His feet were like bronze glowing in a furnace, and His voice was like the sound of rushing waters.

Revelation 1:15

I had a dream wake me up last year with this image and verse about OVERFLOW. I knew I had to paint and share it.

Our God is the provider of impossible overflow. Will we trust Him to do it? Will we daily come to Him to be filled to overflowing? I have heard a wise pastor say, "A cup is not technically full until it is overflowing." I want to be like that. The Lord was gently reminding me that the overflow of our hearts ends up spilling out in our words more than we know, and we can so easily forget the source of our words. There was also an aspect of the dream, that there is a privilege we have to bear His name, operate in His image, and speak with His heart when we are filled by Him.

This piece "Overflow" is a reminder of source. Source of life, provision, and the only place from which those around me need to hear from. There are really only two sources we are filled with, fear or love. Today I extend the invitation to you to ponder the movement and colors of "OVERFLOW". I pray you are swept away as you sense your heart being filled to overflowing with Him.

PRAYER

Thank you, God, for the ability to walk in your Spirit that overflows. Thank you for words of life to those around me that are accessible in your presence and spending time with you. Thank you that I need to receive your good thoughts and thunderous voice of love filling me before I can overflow to others. Help me hear the river of your loving voice today. Thank you, Father.

HEART RESPONSE

- Think of one person who needs an overflowing word of encouragement from the Father today. Spend a minute writing a note to them. Ask God to bring to mind any scripture or words they need to hear about how loved they are. Your overflow can become theirs.

- Simply pay attention to the words you use in the day and where they come from. Notice if they are from a place of love or a place of fear. There is no condemnation.

- If you notice more words are not overflowing from love, just take it as a beautiful and gracious reminder that your well might be dry! Don't worry. God is always "on tap!" Just turn your thoughts to Him and rest in His loving presence, wherever you are. When you see the artwork "Overflow," remember you are surrounded by the source of living water.

you will keep in
perfect
Peace
whose mind is stayed
on you, because he trusts
in you
ISAIAH 26:3

SEPTEMBER

You will keep in perfect peace those whose minds are steadfast, because they trust in you.

Isaiah 26:3

I leave the gift of peace with you-my peace. Not the kind of fragile peace given by the world, but my perfect peace. Don't yield to fear or be troubled in your hearts-instead, be courageous!

John 14:27

Peace, the gift. Peace Himself. There have been books and songs, plaques and pillows made from this idea of peace. This year especially seems to be one that humans are striving for this elusive emotion more than ever. But the good news is, the unearthly good news is, it isn't attainable. Because it isn't just a thing or emotion, it is a person. The Prince of Peace Himself calling out to us on the water. But the struggle is real! Daily the world seeks to dismantle or speak to our hearts and our mind's neuropathways the opposite. I don't know about you, but I am not looking for only a momentary peace. It's so exhausting and elusive. Then we remember to run home to Dad. To turn our hearts back on His face, Peace Himself, and remember He was here all along with us. Peace in us.

A 365-day reality that He came 2,000 years ago and He never really left. The Holy Spirit, the Spirit of Jesus Himself, our gift of solid bedrock Peace is here.

PRAYER

Jesus, thank you. Thank you for coming and never leaving us. Thank you for being our peace. Unveil what clouds our vision of your peace living in us. We choose this day to refocus our hearts on the unseen reality that you are with us, rather than any emotion that steals our focus from this truth. We love You Prince Peace.

HEART RESPONSE

- Spend time journaling how different your day and relationships will be as a result of walking in complete peace.

- Picture Jesus answering for you and walking with you into every space you go. Receive this as your reality in Christ!

GOD is the

strength

of my life and my
portion FOREVER

OCTOBER

My flesh and my heart may fail, but God is the strength of my heart and my portion forever.

Psalm 73:26

And I pray that He would unveil within you the unlimited riches of His glory and favor until supernatural strength floods your innermost being with His divine might and explosive power.

Ephesians 3:16

Do you not know? Have you not heard? The LORD is the everlasting God, the Creator of the ends of the earth. He will not grow tired or weary, and his understanding no one can fathom. He gives strength to the weary and increases the power of the weak. Even youths grow tired and weary, and young men stumble and fall; but those who hope in the LORD will renew their strength. They will soar on wings like eagles; they will run and not grow weary, they will walk and not be faint.

Isaiah 40:28-31

The joy of the LORD is your strength.

Nehemiah 8:10

When was the last time you felt strong? Do you feel strong today? It almost makes me laugh and feel like a child again when I remember God's recipe for giving strength. Joy! What? It seems so ridiculous and impractical. Counter intuitive even. When I am laughing or overwhelmed with joy, my body actually feels vulnerable and physically relaxed, unconsciously pausing for the moment of weakness. Whether it is a deep seated and radical joy in the midst of suffering, or an all-out, doubled over laughter fit, the last word I would use to describe it from the world's perspective would be strength. However, yet again God didn't consult us when He set His heavenly order in place. This takes something like the mind of Christ to rewire my thinking! Surrender to the vulnerability and neediness like a child, to listen for and see my Father's face of love. His loud laughter and joyful acceptance of me as His daughter is what fills me with strength, that the world does not understand. What a unique and unlikely source! I am also incredibly grateful. I do not have to muscle through ANYTHING alone.

HEART RESPONSE

- When did you feel spiritually and emotionally strongest? Looking back at that memory, can you trace back how God's joy over you played a part?

- Surrender any areas you've tried to "muscle" through a situation rather than simply receiving strength in His joyful presence.

- Take a moment to sit with your eyes closed and imagine God, your Father, smiling over you, filling you with His joy like a liquid pouring into your heart. His joy belongs to you.

- Write a prayer of thanks for His strategy for strength.

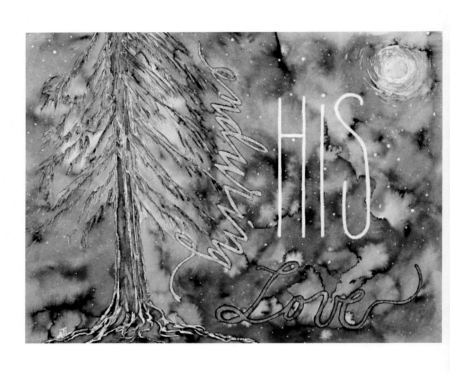

NOVEMBER

Give thanks to the Lord, for he is good.

His love endures forever.

Give thanks to the God of gods.

His love endures forever.

Give thanks to the Lord of lords:

His love endures forever.

To him who alone does great wonders,

His love endures forever.

Who by his understanding made the heavens,

His love endures forever.

Who spread out the earth upon the waters,

His love endures forever.

Who made the great lights-

His love endures forever.

The sun to govern the day,

His love endures forever.

The moon and stars to govern the night;

His love endures forever.

Psalm 136:1-9

For the Lord is good and His love endures forever; His faithfulness continues through all generations.

Psalm 100:5

Now may the Lord move your hearts into *a greater understanding of* God's pure love for you and into Christ's steadfast endurance.

2 Thessalonians 3:5

As the stars in the Psalm reference, this painting uses them to represent the immensity of His love. I also included ancient trees as another familiar symbol of legacy and endurance. Both images are yet weak attempts to capture the understanding of the eternally faithful love of the Father! As humans however, we need help understanding. Thank God He gave us the natural world to reflect His love and speak of His story. That love is strung up on a crisp evening with no clouds to hide the specks of light, or as we gaze vertical leaning against the trunk of a giant redwood tree. Gnarly roots above and below the surface, alive before your great granny and probably long after you are gone. The list could go on and on of lessons from nature.

In this art piece the white and lengthy letters spelling "HIS" stretch across the night scene, drawing attention to His sovereign standing and presence as the central focus. The curving cursive lines wrapping the words "enduring love" are painted as a sturdy chord of rope, reminding us this love is the hope that anchors our souls into eternity with Him.

HEART RESPONSE

- Write or declare out loud a prayer of thanks to God for His faithful love.

- Meditate on how He has been faithful to you over time, even you were unaware of Him.

- Share with your spouse, children, or friend, about His faithfulness as a testimony and encouragement to them.

- Write a song, create a picture, take a photo of something that speaks of His faithful love.

Let Heaven AND nature Sing

ATL

DECEMBER

The heavens declare the glory of God, and the sky above proclaims His handwork. Day to day pours out speech, and night to night reveals knowledge.

There is no speech, nor are there words, whose voice is not heard. Their voice goes out through all the earth, and their words to the end of the world.

Psalm 19:1-4

For unto us a child is born, to us a son is given; and the government shall be upon His shoulder, and His name shall be called Wonderful Counselor, Mighty God, Everlasting Father, Prince of Peace. Of the increase of His government and of peace there will be no end, on the throne of David and over His kingdom, to establish it and to uphold it with justice and with righteousness from this time forth and forevermore. The zeal of the LORD of hosts will do this.

Isaiah 9:6-7

The year says good night and farewell in the month of December. With celebration and sadness, hand in hand, it celebrates Christmas and the birth of Hope Himself. Heaven and nature sing continuously of the Creator and His story. What has God done this year through you, for you, with you, that causes your heart to sing? Where have you seen the Shining One- Jesus, spoken about in Isaiah, show up for you this year? How have you grown in knowing Him as Wonderful Counselor, Mighty God, Everlasting Father, or the Prince of Peace in your life? How do you still long to sing about Him to others in this season? If you haven't a clue how to go about that, just ask him to show you! It could be the best gift you give Him this Christmas.

HEART RESPONSE

- Write down how God showed Himself to you this year, through one of His names mentioned above from Isaiah 9:6.

- Write a song, poem, prayer, or paint a picture thanking Him for who He is and what He means to you. This is a personal gift to your Father in heaven, between the two of you. Know that it means more to Him than you can imagine!

- Make room for more! As this year closes, think of one or two dreams God is already seeding into your heart. If you do not have any coming to mind, just ask Him. Trust that He desires to show you.

- Write down what comes to mind and place it somewhere around your house or car where you will see it often in the coming year.

CONCLUSION

From the bottom of my heart, I hope this little devotional has spurred you on to love and connection with your Maker. I pray that focusing on one image and specific words each month has equipped your days with hope, lit up who He is, and what He has to say about you. May God bless you and may the truth you encountered this year propel you into the next!

Hope inspired,

Allison Teal

To contact Allison or find out more, go to

www.tealpatrickart.com

Facebook or Instagram @tealpatrickart

tealpatrickart@gmail.com

Made in the USA
Middletown, DE
15 March 2021

35307614R00033